Lots to Get

By Carmel Reilly

Lev and Mum hop off the bus.

Mum has a big bag.

Mum and Lev go in.

Mum can see lots of kids.

Lev runs up to the kids.

Lev and Mum get jam buns.

Mum gets a big cup, too.

Mum has a pad
and a red pen.

Mum has lots to get.

Lev and Mum
look for the wok.

Mum got a wok
and a pot and lid.

Lev can see lots of pen kits.

Mum gets a pen kit for Lev.

Mum and Lev go to the bus.

Lev had fun!

CHECKING FOR MEANING

1. What do Lev and Mum get to eat? *(Literal)*
2. What colour is Mum's pen? *(Literal)*
3. Where do you think Mum and Lev were going on the bus at the end of the story? *(Inferential)*

EXTENDING VOCABULARY

lots	Look at the word *lots*. What is the base of this word? What sound does the *s* on the end make? Find some other words in the book where *s* makes the same sound.
to, too	These words sound the same. What is different about the way they are written? What does each of them mean?
wok	Find the word *wok* in the book. What does it mean? What is another word you could use for *wok*?

MOVING BEYOND THE TEXT

1. When have you been shopping? What did you buy?
2. Do you like shopping? Why or why not?
3. Mum used a shopping list in the book. What else can you use a list for?
4. What can you cook in a wok? What other tools might you use for cooking?

SPEED SOUNDS

Kk Ll Vv Qq Ww

Dd Jj Oo Gg Uu

Cc Bb Rr Ee Ff Hh Nn

Mm Ss Aa Pp Ii Tt

PRACTICE WORDS

Lev

lid

lots

wok

kits

kit

kids